ABOUT THE
ONE EARTH BOOKS

During its nearly one hundred years of educating the public about environmental issues, the National Audubon Society has rarely achieved anything as important as reaching out to the world's young people, the voices of tomorrow. For Audubon and its 600,000 members, nothing is so crucial as ensuring that those voices speak in the future on behalf of wildlife.

Audubon reaches out to people in many ways—through its nationwide system of wildlife sanctuaries, through research vital to helping set the nation's environmental policy, through lobbying for sound conservation laws, through television documentaries and fact-based dramatic films, through *Audubon* magazine and computer software, and through ecology workshops for adults and Audubon Adventures clubs in school classrooms. Each of these is critical to reaching a large audience. And now, with the Audubon One Earth books, the environmental community can speak to the youngest minds in our citizenry.

Audubon is proud to publish One Earth in cooperation with Bantam Books. In addition to bringing new information and experiences to young readers, these books will instill in them a fundamental concern for the environment and its decline at the hands of humanity. They will also, it is hoped, stimulate an undying interest in the natural world that will empower young people, as they mature, to protect the world's natural wonders for themselves and for future generations.

We at Audubon hope you will enjoy the One Earth books and that you will find in them an inspiration for joining our earth-saving mission. Young people are the hope for our future.

Christopher N. Palmer
Executive Editor
President, National Audubon
Society Productions

ONE EARTH

WHERE ARE MY PUFFINS, WHALES AND SEALS?

RON HIRSCHI

Photographs by ERWIN and PEGGY BAUER and others

National
Audubon
Society

BANTAM BOOKS · NEW YORK · TORONTO · LONDON · SYDNEY · AUCKLAND

For Erin

If you would like to receive more
information about the National Audubon Society write to:
National Audubon Society, Membership Department,
950 Third Avenue, New York, NY 10022

WHERE ARE MY PUFFINS, WHALES, AND SEALS?
A Bantam Book / October 1992

Executive Editor: Christopher N. Palmer

Library of Congress Cataloging-in-Publication Data
Hirschi, Ron.
     Where are my puffins, whales, and seals? / Ron Hirschi : photographs by Erwin and Peggy Bauer.
     p.   cm.—(One Earth)
  "A National Audubon Society book."
     Summary: Decribes the multitude of life found in and around the sea and how that life is being endangered by marine pollution.
     ISBN 0-553-07803-8.—ISBN 0-553-35472-8 (pbk.)
     1. Marine fauna—Juvenile literature. 2. Puffins—Juvenile literature. 3. Whales—Juvenile literature. 4. Seals (Animals)—
Juvenile literature. 5. Endangered species—Juvenile literature.
[1. Marine animals. 2. Marine pollution. 3. Pollution.]
I. Bauer, Erwin, ill. II. Bauer, Peggy, ill. III. Title. IV. Series: Hirschi, Ron. One Earth.
QL 122.2.H574   1992
591.92—dc20   91-509 CIP AC

Published simultaneously in the United States and Canada

Bantam Books are published by Bantam Books, a division of Bantam Doubleday Dell Publishing Group, Inc. Its trademark,
consisting of the words "Bantam Books" and the portrayal of a rooster, is Registered in U.S. Patent and Trademark Office and in
other countries. Marca Registrada. Bantam Books, 666 Fifth Avenue, New York, New York 10103.

PRINTED IN THE UNITED STATES OF AMERICA

0 9 8 7 6 5 4 3 2 1

INTRODUCTION

Beautiful puffins, majestic whales, and curious seals all help keep the gentle balance of life in the oceans. For centuries we have only taken from the sea. Worse still, we have used the ocean as a place to dump our waste. By harvesting life in the sea as if it has no end, we have driven many animals to extinction. Now our pollution is harming other creatures in the same way.

It is time to give back to the sea in a more thoughtful manner. We can only hope it is not too late to save the balance of life beneath the waves. Join us now as we travel from the places where we live along the Atlantic and Pacific shores to where puffins, whales, seals, and other animals of the sea need our help to save their home.

Walk with me through the harbor streets, past the tourist shops to the busy wharf. Search the shore for a quiet beach and listen to the splashing. Can you hear the voices in the sea?

*G*ulls fly above the pounding surf and hunt for clams, starfish, or snails.

Sandpipers run in and out with each wave, then fly wing to wing up into the sky.

inter loons swim along the shore where water is clean, where air is fresh and salty. But where are my puffins, whales, and seals? They once swam here, too. Then people came with sharp harpoons, speeding boats, and plans that changed the shape of these shores.

Out beyond the beachfront houses, the sea surrounds a rocky island.

Sparkling kelp covers the shore where osyter-catchers poke their bills between the rocks, searching for mussels to open and eat.

Gulls and cormorants build nests on the rough stone ledges. Will puffins raise their babies here, too?

Puffins need islands safe from hungry cats and trampling feet. They lay eggs in burrow nests, tucked safe beneath the ground. From these eggs baby puffins hatch.

But they will survive only where water is free from spilled oil and filled with plenty of fish to eat.

Puffins will raise babies on this island in the sea if we keep it safe. They will fly with their rainbow bills filled with silver fish.

But where are the whales? Can they live here, too?

Watch the distant waters closely for their steaming spout. Pwooosh!

The whale breathes out, then breathes in,

and dives deep, deep beneath the ocean waves.

Nearby, birds called phalaropes swirl on the ocean swells. They stir the water to catch plankton no bigger than your toes. Phalaropes are so small you could hold one in your hand,

yet the biggest of whales will eat the same food
as these tiny birds.

Humpbacks, grays, and giant blue whales—some of which grow bigger than any dinosaur that ever lived on land—eat tons of this food every day.

With the help of caring sea lovers, some whales are finally safe from the hunter's harpoon. Gentle gray whales have recovered and now swim the eastern Pacific.

Will we keep the ocean clean and protect the whale's food to save all the mammals of the sea? Will sleek seals be safe in these waters, too?

Fur seals swim far away from the shore and sleep out on the open sea. They live each day in danger where oil covers the waves and fishing nets entangle their bodies.

Harbor seals swim closer to the shore, sleeping for hours on rocks and even on docks. The seals' friendly faces poke through the emerald green water . . .

where sea otters swim, too.

Curious and playful, the seal might follow your boat if you paddle quietly past.

Leave the seals in their safe hideaway beach. Leave them a quiet and clean place for sleeping, for fishing, and for raising their pups.

Then, next time you listen to the sounds of the ocean, close your eyes and you will hear . . .

the whistling wings of puffins,
the song of the humpback whale,
and the splash of seals.

It is up to us to keep them all
safe at home in the sea.

Afterword

For young readers, parents, teachers,
big brothers, and big sisters:

The sea surrounds us with rich waters offering what once seemed to be limitless harvests of fish, clams, and other food. For centuries, we took its endless bounty for granted and only recently began to realize its limits and problems. The loss of great whales due to commercial whaling is one clear example of how our actions can affect the delicate balance of nature. For some whales, it is already too late. Extinction is a grim reality for many populations, including Atlantic and western Pacific gray whales.

But the comeback of gray whales in the eastern Pacific gives us hope. We must celebrate their return during the past fifty years, learning from this successful protection of an endangered species. If we can save gray whales, we can save other sea creatures, too. We can also learn ways to make the ocean's waters cleaner.

Use of the ocean as a dumping ground for our toxic waste and refuse must end. We urge you to read more about the alternative products you can use and actions you can take as a family and as a community that will prevent toxins from entering waterways leading to the sea. We all live downstream. And the puffins, whales, and seals ultimately receive the cumulative effects of that flow. We are able to decide what we send down to the sea. Let it be clean. Let it be clear.

ACTIVITIES

Things you can do to help you save puffins, whales, seals, and other animals of the sea:

- If you live near the seashore, adopt a beach as a family or school project. Walk the beach often, picking up litter, especially plastic soda-pop rings, fishing line, and other trash that often entangles seabirds and mammals.

- If you live closer to a stream, adopt a section of its banks. Keep it clean, and alert other people to do the same by writing about your efforts in your school or local paper. Imagine, if all our streams were kept clean, the ocean that receives their waters would be much healthier, too.

- Visit a sewage treatment center with your class and find out what happens to our waste.

- Did you know that 71 percent of our planet's surface is made up of oceans? Visit the seashore or an aquarium to find out more about them.

- Learn the language of sea creatures by listening to tapes and records of whale sounds and seabirds. You may be the person, like an archaeologist breaking an ancient language code, to teach the rest of us what the animals of the sea are saying to one another and to us.

- You can also learn more by taking special whale-and puffin-watching boat trips. The National Audubon Society offers many such trips. Contact them directly or call a local travel agent for more information.

About the Author

Ron Hirschi is a renowned environmentalist who worked as a habitat biologist before turning full time to writing and working with children. He now visits children in classrooms and communities nationwide, inspiring their curiosity and helping them to see that there are many things they can do in their own backyards to make our earth a better place.

Ron has written twenty books for children, including the acclaimed *Winter* and *Spring* books and the recently published Discover My World series.

About the Photographers

Erwin and Peggy Bauer and the other contributors are among the world's most highly regarded wildlife photographers. Together the Bauers have published over twenty-five books and countless articles about their worldwide photographic expeditions.

The puffins featured in this book were photographed in the Pribilof Islands and along the coast of Alaska.

Photos of humpback whales were taken at Point Adolphus (Alaska), gray whales were taken in the Pacific Ocean, and blue whales were taken in the Sea of Cortés (California) and the Gulf of Saint Lawrence (Canada).

Harbor seals were photographed along the coast of California and in Prince William Sound (Alaska). Fur seals were photographed on the high seas of the Pacific.